Mel Bay Presents

Mariachi Violin Transcriptions

Arranged by Laura Sobrino

2 3 4 5 6 7 8 9 0

Visit us on the Web at www.melbay.com — E-mail us at email@melbay.com

Table of Contents

La culebra

El llano grande

P.D./arr. Laura Garciacano Sobrino

9

El riflero

16

Jarabe la botella

P.D./arr. Laura Garciacano Sobrino

El jarabe tapatío

P.D./arr. Laura Garciacano Sobrino

Florecitas mexicanas

M. Martínez/arr. L.G. Sobrino

33

Flor de México

36

Lindas pachuqueñas

P.D./arr. Laura Garciacano Sobrino

La marcha zacatecas

G. Godina/arr. Laura Garciacano Sobrino

El zopilote mojado

Laura Garcíacano Sobríno

Laura Garciacano Sobrino was eight years old when she began playing classical violin at her elementary school in Watsonville, California. A 1972 graduate of Aptos High School, Laura was a charter member of the Santa Cruz Country Youth Symphony and enjoyed performing in string quartets. While studying for her B.A. at the University of California, she began exploring the mariachi music world as a semi-professional performer in 1975, making her one of the first women to enter this predominately male genre. Upon completing her studies, she moved to Los Angeles to perform professionally. She became the first woman to play in the groups, *Mariachi Los Galleros de Pedro Rey,* and *Mariachi Sol de Mexico,* both considered among the nations best. Laura Sobrino was also the founding musical director and lead violinist for the all-female mariachi show group, *Mariachi Reyna de los Angeles.* Currently, Mrs. Sobrino is the Musical Director and a violinist for the innovative all-female mariachi show group, *Mariachi Mujer 2000* (www.mariachimujer2000.com). Among her greatest contributions to the mariachi world are her over 25 years of instruction provided to aspiring mariachi musicians, music educators and other professionals both young and old. She has taught in her home, at colleges, music conferences and other professional instructional venues. Mrs. Sobrino is a *National Endowment of the Arts* Master Teacher. Her experiences as mariachi instructor inspired the birth of her publishing company, *Mariachi Publishing* (www.mariachipublishing.com). Her transcriptions have made mariachi music, which for generations was transmitted only by ear, accessible to all. Her transcriptions not only provide a window into the many traditional forms but they also capture authentic mariachi style.

Laura Sobrino lives in Whittier, CA with her husband Dan (www.sobrino.net), and their children Nicte and Nazul.

Made in the USA
Middletown, DE
20 October 2015